A MOTHER'S HEART

Memoir of a Special Needs Parent

It can be lonely parenting a special needs child,
but you are not alone.

EICHIN CHANG-LIM

A MOTHER'S HEART

Copyright © 2017 by Eichin Chang-Lim

All Rights Reserved

No part of this publication may be reproduced, distributed, or transmitted in any form or by any means, including photocopying, recording, or other electronic or mechanical methods, without the prior written permission of the publisher, except in the case of brief quotations embodied in critical reviews and certain other noncommercial uses permitted by copyright law.

Although every precaution has been taken to verify the accuracy of the information contained herein, the author and publisher assume no responsibility for any errors or omissions. No liability is assumed for damages that may result from the use of information contained within.

Some names and identifying details have been changed to protect the privacy of individuals.

www.eichinchanglim.com

Edited by Susan Hughes
Copy Edited by Eeva Lancaster
Cover Design and Formatting by
The Book Khaleesi

ISBN-13: 978-1545264201
ISBN-10: 1545264201

TABLE OF CONTENTS

PROLOGUE 1

CHAPTER 1 3

When in Doubt, Check it Out

CHAPTER 2 13

It's Okay to Cry

CHAPTER 3 21

A Support System is Crucial: Family, Support Group, or Psychological Counseling

CHAPTER 4 29

Early Intervention: A Race for Time

CHAPTER 5 35

Sibling Involvement

CHAPTER 6 51

Spouse Communication

CHAPTER 7 59

　Motherhood vs. Career

CHAPTER 8 69

　Choosing the Right Special Education Placement

CHAPTER 9 91

　Social Skills Development

CHAPTER 10 101

　Working with School and Resource Teachers

CHAPTER 11 111

　Surviving the Teenage Years

CHAPTER 12 121

　Genetic Counseling and Sex Education

CHAPTER 13 129

　Occupational Choices

CHAPTER 14 137

Time to Let Go

CHAPTER 15 147

It's Okay if Things Don't Turn Out as You Expected

CHAPTER 16 155

Motherhood Never Ends. Give Yourself a Pat on the Back

About the Author 163

Other Books by Eichin Chang-Lim

FLIPPING: An Uplifting Novel of Love

Love, A Tangled Knot (2017)

Acknowledgements

Special thanks to author John Dolan; this book would not exist without your encouragement and guidance in the initial stage. Huge thanks to author Bob Boyd; you labored through my first draft and provided me candid and insightful critique. Much appreciation to Susan Hughes; your editing brings the story to life.

The entire content of this manuscript has been read and consented upon by my family. Thank you for your support throughout the process. Especially to Victoria; thank you for taking the time to share your experience in the Sibling chapter in the midst of your stressful schedule.

For all the parents, families, friends, health care providers, educators, and administrators who help a child requiring special attention reach their full potential.

PROLOGUE

Sometimes, there's an unexpected anguish lurking behind something that we initially perceived as "perfect." Life is filled with situations like this. It throws us a curveball, and all we can do is find a way to catch it and not drop the ball. Ultimately, we discover the joy, love, and beauty in the midst of distress.

I am writing this book based on my personal experience as the mother of a child rendered profoundly deaf due to a genetic disorder, and as an optometrist who, through my years of practice, had encountered children with various degrees of visual impairment due to congenital disabilities or unforeseen incidents. I am neither a child psychologist nor a family counselor. It is my desire to share my experiences with other mothers raising children in need of special attention, in hopes that they may find inspiration, encouragement, and joy in the process.

It can be lonely raising a special needs child, but you are not alone.

CHAPTER 1

When in Doubt, Check it Out

"Life is the art of living with uncertainty, without being paralyzed by fear."

~ Dr. W. Dillon

According to the Center for Disease Control and Prevention, around 1 in every 33 babies is born with a congenital disorder. Some congenital disorders can be identified immediately. For example, Down syndrome can exhibit various degrees of characteristics upon birth. Others, though, are subtle and hard to detect until later.

In some congenital disorders, like Juvenile Macular Degeneration, symptoms will not manifest themselves until the teenage years or early adulthood. Either way, it is critical to investigate the problem fully when you feel "something is not quite right" about your child's development or behavior.

♥ Eichin's Story ♥

I was pregnant with my son Theodore, whom we call Teddy, during my fourth year of optometry school, and he was born a week after my California State Board of Examination for Optometry. I had to travel 400 miles to the University of California, Berkeley, for the two days of testing. My obstetrician prescribed a medication to prevent me from having contractions and giving birth during the traveling and examinations. I also developed severe dermatitis and had to take an antihistamine. My labor lasted twenty-four hours, and Teddy was born by cesarean section. He weighed over eight pounds and had ten fingers and ten toes, so he was perfect in every way. His most noticeable feature at birth was his sky-blue eyes.

Some people asked us, "So, you put blue opaque contact lenses on your baby?" Others wondered, "Can an Asian couple, both with dark-brown eyes, have a blue-eyed baby?" We even heard, "Who was the mailman?" whispered behind our backs.

Once I brought Teddy home from the hospital, I noticed that he could sleep through the noise of the vacuum cleaner, and loud laughter during family gatherings didn't wake him. "What a great baby with a nice temperament!" friends and relatives commented with envy.

However, a small, disturbing voice grew louder within me. I expressed my concerns to his pediatrician at his sixth-month well-baby checkup. The pediatrician shook a rattle near

Teddy's head, and when the baby turned toward the sound, the doctor dismissed my concerns. I obsessively repeated the test at home, but Teddy turned his head too inconsistently to quell my fears.

At his ninth-month well-baby checkup, I raised my concerns again. I begged and pleaded with his pediatrician. "I don't think he can hear!" I repeated the same line over and over, unable to vocalize the word *deaf*.

He gave in and referred me to a pediatric neurologist. Teddy's brainstem auditory evoked response (BAER) test was performed in a university hospital lab on a beautiful spring afternoon. I was in the fourth month of my second pregnancy, exhausted and cranky. Fortunately, my husband volunteered to be the driver that day.

At the end of the test, the neurologist told us, "If he were my child, I would not worry about it." My husband turned and winked at me with a look that said, *See? I told you. You are being neurotic.*

Being right was not my goal; all I wanted was to know the truth. I constantly checked my textbooks. Yes, call me obsessive, if you like. I understood the various milestones a baby needed to reach. At six months, Teddy made babbling noises, but, by nine months, the babblings had stopped. He had become completely silent. There were times when he seemed to be in his own world, playing with his toys, undisturbed by the surrounding noises. Wanting so badly to believe he was okay, I talked to him, played music to him, sang to him, and taught him to say, "Mommy" and "Daddy." Teddy blinked his brilliant blue eyes, smiled at me, and imitated my mouth movements, but no sound came out.

I pushed the stroller and walked like a penguin into the pediatrician's office for his one-year well-baby checkup. Because I hadn't given my uterus a break between pregnancies, I looked like I was having twins, but I didn't care. In tears, I shared my concerns with the pediatrician again, begging him to listen. He glanced at my well-expanded tummy and nodded like a bobblehead. This time, he referred Teddy to an audiologist.

It was a month before my second baby was due, a hot and dry September day in Southern California. Teddy could not walk yet. I did not have lap space for him to sit on, so my husband had to hold him while they did the sound test in a well-controlled sound booth. Then, the audiologist performed a second BAER test. Afterward, he had us sit in his office while he studied the results. His diploma and credentials were displayed on the wall: impressive and intimidating. As we waited for his pronouncement, the time seemed to stretch into eternity. The air conditioning blasted, and I hugged my arms tight across my chest, unsure if the chill I felt was from the cold, or my apprehension.

Finally, the audiologist came in and sat down in front of us.

The verdict was, "Your son is profoundly deaf," he said. "Teddy has the so-called corner audiogram. He could possibly feel the vibration better than hear the sound." Then, to make his point, he rephrased it again. "With the degree of his hearing loss, do not expect him to call you Mommy or Daddy in words." He handed us some pamphlets and copies of resource information.

The reality hurt, as if someone stuck a sharp knife right into my chest. Although the diagnosis was not a shocker, I was still sad and angry. I was angry that the whole universe did not show a shred of remorse for my son's deafness. I was angry that my husband seemed so calm and in control. I was angry that I blamed myself for my son's disability. I should not have studied so thoroughly for my board exam; I had stressed the fetus, and that's why he's deaf.

It was a month of chaos between the diagnosis of Teddy's deafness and my second child's birth. Teddy was referred to a children's hospital for a complete checkup to rule out other diseases associated with his deafness. One specialist visit led to another. Finally, we knew the solution to the mystery surrounding his blue eyes. He had a genetic condition called *Waardenburg Syndrome*, which was the cause of both his hearing loss and his eye color.

CHAPTER 2

It's Okay to Cry

"Crying doesn't mean you're weak. Since birth, it's been a sign that you're alive."

~Unknown

We all have dreams. Inevitably, we impose our dreams on our offspring subconsciously. Some people dream of being a professional athlete, a successful musician, or a person of influence in an academic, business, or political arena. Others just dream about having a simple, peaceful life. At the least, we want our children to be able to live independently, enjoy everyday life, and contribute as a member of society.

When a child doesn't turn out as expected, we see their bright future instantly turn dim. As parents, we may be bombarded with questions and uncertainties. Dreams are shattered; worries set in. We feel isolated from other parents who have "perfect" children. The sympathy of others, while well-intentioned, becomes an extra weight on our already-heavy hearts. It has nothing to do with whether or not we accept our unexpected gift; it is about how to accept the reality wholeheartedly. The acceptance of reality takes time, and the transition period can be confusing. You may switch back and forth between being optimistic and dejected.

♥ Eichin's Story ♥

I filled my days with doctors' visits and tons of phone calls to check out various institutes during the month between Teddy's diagnosis and my daughter's birth. I told myself, "That's what a good mother should do. A good mother should be strong for her child, and I am a good mother." My tears flowed at first, but I suppressed them quickly. "If I want my son to be strong to overcome his birth defect, I should demonstrate my strength to him," I thought to myself.

A month went by. I gave birth to a daughter, again through cesarean section. We named her Victoria. There was no mandatory newborn hearing screening test in California then. Since Teddy's diagnosis was still fresh, her pediatrician recommended that she have BAER testing, just to rule out the slim possibilities. Coincidentally, the same pediatric neurologist who had tested Teddy a few months before and proclaimed his hearing perfect, was appointed to perform the test on my one-day-old daughter. He reported to her pediatrician that she showed some degree of hearing loss as well.

Right then... I completely lost it.

My obstetrician ordered a psychiatrist to come to my maternity room to evaluate my condition and prescribe medication to calm me down. He was partially bald and a bit overweight. I could see his beer belly bulging against his white coat. I'm not sure why his appearance stands out in my mind, even today.

Apparently, he had retrieved my case history

from the hospital staff. He said, "Fortunately, I have four normal children, but birth defects can happen."

I picked up a cup from a nearby stand and threw it at him. "Go to hell!" I yelled. Luckily for him, I was still in pain from the cesarean section; otherwise, I would have jumped down from the bed and strangled him.

Upon his swift exit, he turned around and said, "You need a good cry."

He told the nurse, "Let her cry, if that happens."

With that, the dam broke and I started to cry. I cried my heart and guts out. I cried for my misfortune. I cried for my baby's uncertain future. Later on, I learned through reading articles that crying is a natural part of the healing process. My experiences have taught me that we need to cry to gain real strength, and it is okay to do so.

As it turned out, my daughter's hearing was normal. We found out as soon as we brought her home, because she was startled by sudden noises, like the sound of the doorbell.

My relief cannot be explained.

CHAPTER 3

A Support System is Crucial: Family, Support Group, or Psychological Counseling

"Although the world is full of suffering, it is also full of the overcoming of it."

~Helen Keller

It can be lonely raising a child who needs extra attention. No matter how strong a person appears, we all have our vulnerabilities. Raising a child with special needs is a long-term responsibility and a stressful job. There are times when you wonder whether you can make it through another day, and depression often sets in. Negative voices intrude into your thoughts. You feel as if you're trapped in a dark tunnel and will never escape. We need support to sustain our strength. We need someone to offer us a helping hand and walk with us through the dark valley.

♥ Eichin's Story ♥

I have to admit that I had difficulty breaking the news to the family. I thought it was culture-related, but I found out later, it's not just an Asian thing. As expected, they could not conceal their disappointment when I told them. My mother-in-law's response was, "How? There is no history of deafness on my side of the family." My dad's a perfectionist; he was sad. My mother cried and hid the news from my relatives back home. Her excuse was that it did not matter to them, so why bother? Please don't get me wrong; I knew they all loved my son. It was just hard for them to digest the news right away. It takes time for the shock to fade, to transform into something positive that the family can rally behind. They were concerned about how other people would judge a child with a birth defect. Family support would come later, but it initially felt like the boat was sinking.

I shared my troubles with my closest friends, colleagues, and church members, and they provided comfort and support. They helped me see things from different perspectives. It gave me a sense of stability when someone said, "You are in my prayers." I am not a person who finds it easy to pick up the phone and talk to someone, especially to ask for prayers or support. Now, thinking about it, I should have done so more often.

The biggest struggle for me was coping with the jealousy and anguish I felt whenever I saw little boys around Teddy's age talking their heads off. I could not help but feel envious and angry. I would think, *It's not fair*.

I think the best support came from talking with parents who were in the same situation. The school Teddy attended then had a physiologist/family counselor who would come in to meet with parents once a month. We met together to talk about our kids and our difficulties with their schooling, and in our daily lives. We were not embarrassed to share our fear, jealousy, anguish, and guilt. We sighed, we cried, and we managed to find something to joke and laugh about.

The ability to understand what others were going through, and the sense that we were all "in the same boat" was imperative. Since every symptom and condition has a broad range of severity and affects the progress of each child differently, we refrained from competing and comparing with one another. We cheered for even the smallest progress or milestones for each other's kids. I remember how light and grateful I felt after those meetings. We developed strong bonds. I still keep in touch with some of those parents, even after our kids moved on to different schools and colleges.

My advice to other parents is this: Do not be reclusive. Reach out to parents in a similar situation, and lend your hand and shoulders to others. You gain strength by giving others support.

Also, do not let the initial "blame game" of your family members consume you. Do not bury yourself in the self-pity trap for too long. They are normal parts of the process. Recognize it, let it go quickly, and move on. Your child needs positive energy from you as soon as possible. Time is of the essence.

CHAPTER 4

Early Intervention: A Race for Time

"There is no debate or doubt: early intervention is your child's best hope for the future."

~Autism Speaks

The first few years of a child's life is considered a critical period. A child needs to have sufficient stimuli for all their senses to develop normally. However, a child with a disability may be deprived of or block the stimuli. It's essential to have a professionally designed educational program intervene at the earliest age possible, to narrow the gap of the developmental delay. Ask the school district or the child's pediatrician for resources. In the meantime, do not let the professionals limit your child's ability. Have faith in your child's ultimate potential.

♥ Eichin's Story ♥

Vision and hearing are two major parts of our sensory system. I applied my knowledge of vision therapy to Teddy's deafness training. Although the prognosis the audiologist gave us was grim, I decided to have the most powerful hearing aids fitted on him as soon the diagnosis was confirmed. I refused to back off, even though the audiogram showed Teddy had only a meager amount of residual hearing, and the chances of him ever communicating orally was slim. I hoped that the powerful hearing aids would provide some stimuli to his auditory cortex, the part of the brain responsible for his hearing.

The hearing aids appeared humongous on his tiny ears. We had to use loops and surgical tape to secure them. Another struggle was keeping the hearing aids on him all the time. He would pull them off with all his strength, and throw them on the floor. We ended up having two sets of hearing aids—one to use and another as a spare.

Once he had the hearing aids on, we made sure he received sufficient sound stimuli. We sat him on our laps and read children's books to him, directly into his hearing aids. As if with a normal child, I sat him on my lap and played piano to him. He wormed around, and I let him bang on the piano keys. I talked to him nonstop. I did not care whether he heard me or not. I just kept talking, singing, playing music, and reading to him. I assumed he could hear me.

One incident struck a chord in me. One day, not long after Teddy's diagnosis, I talked to a lady about deaf education in general, and she asked me, "Do you know what the sign language is for the word *black*?"

"No." I looked at her in puzzlement. "Tell me." I did not know any sign language then.

She straightened her right index finger and moved the tip across her forehead.

"Do you know why?" She paused for a few beats, and I shook my head.

"Because deaf people, on average, have a fourth-grade reading level. The only job they used to be able to manage was as miners. They'd wipe their sweat with a dirty hand and leave a black mark on their forehead."

I decided to focus my efforts on developing Teddy's reading skills at an early age. He had always performed above his grade level in reading, based on standardized testing. He and Victoria were voracious readers.

Here's a thought to share: Read to your kids and play music to them as early as possible, regardless of their physical, mental, or intelligence levels. Good books and music are part of most early interventions, and they could carry a person a long way.

CHAPTER 5

Sibling Involvement

"I don't believe an accident of birth makes people sisters or brothers. It makes them siblings, gives them mutuality of parentage. Sisterhood and brotherhood is a condition people have to work at."

~Maya Angelou

As parents, our goal is to treat our children in an impartial, consistent manner, despite their differences. Having a special needs child in the family certainly tilts the scales, no matter how hard you try to avoid it. In reality, we love each child differently in our own special way. My grandmother used to apply an analogy to illustrate this. She would open her hands out and say, "See? Your thumb and four fingers are all different in length. Yet, it hurts the same when you bite each one of them." In Chinese, the words *hurt* and *love* sound exactly the same. Please don't ask me why you'd want to bite your fingers!

I think it's important to listen and talk to the other children openly and honestly. They are facing their own challenges as well. They can struggle with feelings of loneliness, guilt, unfairness, embarrassment, and helplessness, because of their special needs sibling.

Later in this chapter, Victoria will share her story of growing up with a deaf brother.

♥ Eichin's Story ♥

Since Victoria was born one month after Teddy's hearing impairment diagnosis, we really could not pinpoint when and how she realized that Teddy was different from other kids. I used to put them on either side of me while I did auditory-speech training for Teddy. We put them on our laps to read to them at the same time. Victoria learned to speak at an early age because of this. During their toddler years, when others had difficulties understanding Teddy, Victoria would interpret for him. She would talk to Teddy and communicate with him just as she did with other kids, yet they fought fiercely at times because of their closeness in age.

They were both in after-school programs

when they reached preschool age. I got called in by a program director from time to time when fighting occurred, but by then, the situation always involved other kids bullying or teasing Teddy. Victoria would get furious, yelling, "He's my brother! Want to fight?" Then, Teddy would step in to protect his petite sister, and the fighting continued.

One time, we were at a supermarket, and a boy stared openly at Teddy for too long. Victoria glared back at him and said, "What are you looking at? He's my brother!" This situation went on for years. Victoria was a feisty, petite girl protecting her brother from being discriminated against or bullied. Teddy guarded Victoria with a fierce loyalty to prevent anyone from beating her up in the process.

I know Victoria loves Teddy deeply, but she had her moments. She threw herself on the sofa one day after school, sobbing. She was in junior high then. She did not want to tell me at first, but finally, she muttered, "Why can't I have a normal brother like everyone else?" It must have been difficult for her to verbalize those feelings, but I knew someone must have hurt her terribly.

Victoria and Teddy attended the same junior and senior high school. They were on the same tennis team, and they shared quite a few friends through the years. They read similar books. The thing I enjoyed the most, during which I always stood aside and let them be themselves, was listening to them discuss and debate a book they had just read. They would discuss the plot, the characters, and the author's writing style. Sometimes they agreed with each other; other times they disagreed and argued wholeheartedly. Teddy's speech is understandable, but it is not perfect. Victoria would correct his speech candidly in an inoffensive way. Of course, they continued to fight just as normal siblings did. But it was over silly things, like food.

They went to different colleges. Ted stayed in Southern California; Victoria left for Northern California, four hundred miles away. They communicated with each other more frequently than with their parents. If we wanted to know about one of them, we just asked the other one. That's how things were.

They loved each other. They knew how to push each other's buttons. They were—and are—siblings.

Note: For those special needs children who

have no siblings, it is advisable to develop a deep relationship with close family members, like cousins, or a friend. One of Teddy's best friends was an only child. His mother repeatedly expressed her gratitude for his friendship with Teddy. The supportive relationship takes time and requires parental guidance.

♥ Victoria's Story ♥

My brother and I are very close and have been for most of our lives. He is one year older, but I always felt like I had to be the responsible one for both of us. This is not because of his hearing impairment, but rather because he was a typical boy growing up. He would do things like forget to turn in his homework, play too many video games, eat tons of food then leave a mess, or joke around and pull pranks on others. I always knew Ted was intelligent, funny, and a normal kid overall.

Sometimes, I did feel protective of him because of his disability. It bothered me the most when other people would judge him. Some couldn't get past the extra effort Ted had to put in to communicate, or his visible hearing devices. In a way, I became his advocate. Whenever we met new people, I felt the need to explain his hearing situation to them. In stores, restaurants, or when hanging out with friends, I made sure people understood him and he understood others. His processor is unable to pick apart multiple conversations going on at the same time, so he would feel left out in group settings. Though I wasn't always around, when we were together, it was something I was aware of, and I would try to make sure he felt included.

Ted has had an interesting life journey. There were definitely countless moments when he felt different, or struggled to converse with others but gave up because of the huge amount of effort it took. Fortunately, he managed to have a solid group of friends for many years when he was younger. It helped that many of them continued on to the same middle and high school together.

I have to commend my parents for spending so much effort getting him involved in team sports and other activities in order to make friends. My brother was a gamer, and even though I know my parents did not think video games were the most useful way to spend your time, they let him stay up-to-date with games, because it was his way of connecting with his friends. Some of these things make me laugh, now that I think about it. For example, they would have LAN parties where all the boys would lug their entire desktop computers to one person's house and spend the night playing games like *Counterstrike* while eating pizza. He and I did share many friends, so even though we fought a lot, we also spent a decent amount of time together growing up.

When Ted left for college, things changed. He was in a completely new environment, and it wore on him. Making friends was at times a nightmare. Every class was hard, because he could not understand the lecturing professors. By the end of his first year, he withdrew from social life and spent most of his hours online, communicating with others on *World of Warcraft*. By escaping online, he could talk with others perfectly by typing into chats and messages. No one knows you're disabled online.

Things got worse, and his grades dropped. I knew that he did not feel like he belonged anywhere and didn't know what he wanted to do with his life. Directionless, he ended up taking time off from UC Irvine to check out another school that had a high number of deaf students. Unfortunately, the Deaf community is quite different from those who are raised with the auditory-verbal method of communicating. Yet again, Ted didn't feel like he belonged.

He came back to UCI, and my parents forced him to give up gaming because it was destroying his grades. It was quite a struggle, but when he finally quit, he fell into a depression. None of us could have predicted that, but it makes sense in hindsight. It had essentially cut him off from most of his friends and his social life. Luckily, Ted lived with a roommate, and he and his friends reached out to Ted to bring him through this rough time.

Throughout all this, Ted and I stayed close by texting and talking online. I was hundreds of miles away, but we still felt like a significant part of each other's life because we would share personal thoughts or ask advice from each other, that we would not share with anyone else. When he was going through these lows, or when I was struggling, we always knew we would be there for each other and do anything we could to help.

After that, Ted somehow managed to over-rebound and became somewhat over the top with his social life and the dating game. The stories I could tell! Of course, I won't, but they are really hilarious. Ted has since evened out, and I would dare say he is as well-adjusted as the next person. He has finally discovered his true career passion of becoming a physical therapist, is in a great relationship, and has many friends in real life.

All my years with Ted had given me so much more insight into the silent health struggles that others go through, and he is one of the reasons I am finishing medical school to become a physician. He and I are extremely grateful to my parents, who researched to find specialized hearing impairment schools for Ted when he was young, fought to get him cochlear implant surgeries, and spent years paying speech therapists to work with him.

Growing up with Ted has been quite an experience, but I would not change our relationship for anything. Yes, he stressed my parents out for years, because they were worried about his future. Yes, he and I argued many times. Of course, it would be better if he did not have to go through a lifetime of difficulties most people don't have to experience. However, in the end, life is what it is, and you have to make the best of it. We are thankful for everything he has. I am just a sister who loves her brother unconditionally and would do anything for him.

CHAPTER 6

Spouse Communication

"When you make the sacrifice in marriage, you're sacrificing not to each other but to unity in a relationship."

~Joseph Campbell

I'd like to share this statement with you, which I found at the American Psychological Association's website.

> *"Marriage and divorce are both common experiences. In Western cultures, more than 90 percent of people marry by age 50. Healthy marriages are good for a couple's mental and physical health. They are also good for children; growing up in a happy home protects children from mental, physical, educational and social problems. However, about 50 percent of married couples in the United States divorce. The divorce rate for subsequent marriages is even higher."*

We all wish marriages could be like Disney movies that end happily ever after. In reality, it requires much effort to keep a marriage moving forward smoothly. Any unfavorable factors or events can tip the scale. Having a child with a genetic disorder or special needs is one of them.

♥ Eichin's Story ♥

I remember attending one support meeting conducted by a family psychologist specifically for couples with hearing-impaired children. She said the divorce rate for families with a special needs child is substantially higher than the average. I can't recall the exact figures she presented; however, it did not sound hopeful at all. She endeavored to impress and prepare us mentally and psychologically for the challenges involved in having a special needs child.

My husband and I separated twice during the course of our marriage. We had issues, and the marriage was a challenge. Don't get me wrong; my husband is a good man and a wonderful father. But there are many elements involved in a marriage, as in any kind of relationship. Marriage is a complicated and meandrous journey, and when you're parenting a special needs child, there are more than the usual number of bumps in the road.

At the time of our first separation, our kids had just started elementary school. It was extremely confusing and difficult for them. I could not bear to see them suffer, so we went through counseling and tried to make it work. Four years later, we separated again. The kids were older, but it wasn't any easier for them. They were frightened because they didn't know what would happen next. They acted out at home and stumbled at school. I realized that I would never be genuinely happy if my kids suffered from a failed marriage. I told my husband that my goal was to provide our kids with a secure and stable environment during their childhood years. Basically, we put all our issues aside and focused on the kids. We avoided arguing in front of them. Did they sense the tension between their parents? Of course, they did; and they learned to play "Mommy said, Daddy said" games.

Despite many conflicts and differences between us, we held fast to our goal—to provide our kids with a stable home—for we knew that was one of the key factors in helping them reach their full potential. It was an easy thing to say, but not an easy thing to do. There were times when I wondered whether all the effort we were putting in was worth it, but we made it through.

Few years ago, our daughter graduated from UC Berkeley and was accepted into medical school. We helped her settle into a new apartment and attended her white coat ceremony. Teddy was also there. As we were taking photos after the ceremony, Victoria turned to us, beaming in her symbolic white coat, and said, "Mom and Dad, Teddy and I want to thank you for staying together so we did not have to go through family dramas as many of our friends did." I knew she meant it. It made all our efforts worthwhile.

I am neither a marriage counselor nor a psychologist, and I don't intend to influence anyone in staying in a miserable marriage, or remain married just for the sake of the kids. Marriage is hard, with or without children, and divorce is not a decision to be made lightly. I know marriage is not one rosy shade of pink all the time—could it be more than fifty shades? Possibly! No relationship is perfect, even between two people with good intentions.

One thing I do know is that divorce has a major impact on the children involved. So, too, does a family life filled with discord, unhappiness, and broken promises. It's a tough decision to make, and what worked for our family might not be the best solution for others.

CHAPTER 7

Motherhood vs. Career

*"Motherhood has a very humanizing effect.
Everything gets reduced to essentials."*

~Meryl Streep

According to the recent census, the data showed that nearly seventy percent of mothers were classified as "Working Mothers." Why does a mother have to work outside the home? There are many reasons, and they vary from one individual to the next. "How to balance motherhood and career" is always a subject of interest; you frequently find articles on the topic in women's magazines and professional journals. Numerous books have been written about it. Even academic institutions have done research on it. You can read all of them and still be uncertain about whether you are doing the right thing at the end of the day. You are stressed as a working mother, and you feel guilty for having to leave your kids with a sitter or at after-school programs. I applaud all stay-at-home mothers. We know stay-at-home mothers actually work harder, in many respects, than those who are employed outside the home. Motherhood is a career in itself, even though some people don't recognize it as such.

♥ Eichin's Story ♥

As I mentioned earlier, Teddy was born one week after my California State Board exam. It took more than two months for me to receive my license. My classmates were waiting in anguish, but not me. I immersed myself in the role of brand-new mother; I enjoyed every second of it. Holding an infant in my arms and nursing him was the most thrilling and fulfilling feeling I have ever experienced. It was magical.

In the meantime, my husband had a contract ready to sign to purchase an existing practice from a retiring doctor. It had always been his dream to own a practice and be his own boss. The day we received our licenses, he officially took over the practice, and I received a phone call for a job interview. My husband had sent out job applications for me while I was busy with our newborn. I went to the interview half-heartedly, and was offered the position right on the spot. I cried all the way home, but they were not joyful tears. I did not want the job. I wanted to stay home with my son. Leaving my infant boy in someone's care was difficult. Yet, I knew it was logical for me to work full time. We had a combined $130,000 of student loans, plus my husband's business loan. It was the right thing for me to work full time in a corporate setup, with a stable, consistent paycheck, plus health and dental benefits for the family.

One year later, my daughter was born. I was offered a Managing Doctor position right after returning from maternity leave. I let my supervisor know up front how my son's hearing impairment and my newborn baby might affect my work. The regional manager was a kind individual. He promised to assign me in a location close to home, if I accepted the position. I liked the idea that my work would only be three miles away from home, and only about one mile from the kids' prospective schools. Deep inside, I knew it was a necessity to have the health care insurance the job would provide for my family. My husband was self-employed, and my son's deafness was considered a pre-existing condition. Plus, it was hard to get private insurance then. So, I accepted the position.

While seeking direction for my son's deaf education, I endeavored to become proficient in my new job's responsibilities: performing eye examinations throughout the day, managing the practice to ensure its growth and smooth operation, reading monthly profit/loss statements, hiring and terminating workers, inventory control, loss prevention, business/manpower planning, basic human resource laws, and staff training.

Once I accepted the reality that both my husband and I needed to work full time, we came up with a schedule. I took two weekdays off and worked through the weekends, and he took care of the kids on weekends. The first few years, we relied on family members and a nanny to take care of them for the remaining three days; then, we placed them in after-school programs when they grew older.

The two weekdays off were essential for me. I used those days to run errands, take the kids to doctors' visits, attend IEP meetings/teacher conferences, and carpooled with other parents. This schedule lasted until they both left home for college.

The insurance had been invaluable, as Teddy had five invasive surgical procedures during his growing-up years.

We resolved the health insurance issue once the kids had student insurance through their colleges, and I quit my corporate job. My husband had persuaded me to join his practice, which was much farther from home. It has worked out fine, so far. I continue to enjoy the eye care profession. I see it as a privilege to examine peoples' eyes, which are the windows to their souls. It also gives me the flexibility to pursue my other passions, which I have been dreaming about for years.

Of course, I am sharing all these experiences

with you in hindsight. I have to confess that there was turmoil during the process. I was repeatedly advised by other professionals that a mother should stay home with her special needs child if she wanted to bring out the kid's best potential. That statement was threatening, and it impacted my sanity from time to time. The guilty feelings were the hardest to cope with; I could not help but wonder whether I was doing the right thing. One thing I learned through the years was that I needed to focus on the moment and the people around me. It was detrimental to my well-being if I wondered about my kids while at work, or worried about my job while at home.

We all have to make decisions based on the circumstances. Motherhood vs. career was one of them. What was right for my family and me, might not be what works best for you and yours.

Just do your research, study the options, and follow your heart.

CHAPTER 8

Choosing the Right Special Education Placement

"Every child should have the opportunity to receive quality education."

~Bill Frist

To most people, it sounds logical to provide special education for a special needs child. What's the big deal? Normal kids receive "normal" education; special needs kids receive "special" education. In reality, it's not so straightforward. Those who are familiar with special education will know the terms inclusion, mainstreaming, segregation, and exclusion. Parents with a special needs child can get overwhelmed, confused, and frustrated. You obtain information from various resources, all with good intentions, but many times, they are contradictory to one another. You wade through the options, determined to provide the best educational opportunities for your child, but you're not certain whether you made the right decision.

♥ Eichin's Story ♥

I thought of Helen Keller right after Teddy's diagnosis. Helen Keller had a teacher, Ann Sullivan, to enlighten her and navigate her through her early years, which led to her ultimate success. However, I really did not have a clear idea of what I was looking for at that time. The audiologist and pediatrician gave me pamphlets and booklets. The smiling faces on the covers were a bit irritating. I was introduced to the concept of "Deaf culture."

The Deaf community is a close-knit society; I discovered that rather quickly. They spell the word *Deaf* with a capital *D*, as opposed to the dictionary spelling of the word in relation to hearing impairment. The members of the Deaf community tend to view deafness as a variation of the human experience, rather than a disability. They value their unique means of communication—sign language. If you are deaf but don't use sign language, you and your entire family are outcast from the Deaf community. Basically, the Deaf community believes that you do not accept yourself as a unique individual if you are deaf and don't sign. The family bears the guilt for that, as well.

I realized the diversity of deaf education once I visited the deaf schools. I discovered there's more than one kind of sign language in the USA. Actually, there are hundreds of sign languages worldwide. The most common one in this country is the American Sign Language (ASL). Then, I was told that Signing Exact English (SEE) is superior to ASL, because it required deaf kids to sign exactly the same as spoken English, and follow written English grammatically. According to the SEE supporters, the deaf kids with SEE training had better writing skills and higher educational achievements. Another approach to deaf education is called "total communication," which incorporates several modes of communication—sign, oral, auditory and others—and cued speech.

At that time, only a few institutes were geared for an entirely oral education for the deaf. One of them was the John Tracy Clinic, located in downtown Los Angeles. The John Tracy Clinic was established by actor Spencer Tracy and his wife, Louise, when their son, John, was diagnosed with profound deafness. The John Tracy Clinic teaches kids to learn lip-reading and speaking.

Just a few days before Victoria's due date,

while at my OBGYN's office for a checkup, a nurse who still had a fresh memory about Teddy's birth gave me a phone number.

"Why don't you call this school in Whittier?" she said, "They might have a retired teacher who could work with your son."

When I got home, I did just that. The person answered the phone enthusiastically and invited me to visit the school. I sighed. My frustration and confusion were beyond words by this time. *Was it worth the drive over there with my ready-to-pop tummy?* I was exhausted.

Teddy was not walking yet. Moving him from the infant car seat in my Honda Civic to a stroller was something I dreaded. After some pondering, I grabbed his diaper bag, picked him up, and headed to Whittier, a small city southeast of Los

Angeles.

The school was located inside a church. Pushing him through the long hallway, I was a bit apprehensive as I stopped by the administration office. The secretary took me to meet with the school director shortly thereafter. She gave me a warm welcome and looked at Teddy. "What a kid! He reminds me of the cute boy in *The Last Emperor*." I hadn't seen that movie, but I assumed she was giving him a compliment.

She took me on a tour from classroom to classroom. All the kids were wearing hearing aids. In one classroom, five kids of preschool age were dancing to the music.

"Are you listening to the music? Move your body with the music. Let's dance, everyone," the teacher said, dancing along with them.

I noticed immediately that the children in that program had nearly "normal," beautiful voices. Their speech was intelligible—not perfect, but easy to understand. Their voices grasped my interest and attention. I pointed that out to the director.

She briefly shared with me the program's philosophy: "We teach our children to learn to talk by listening with whatever residual hearing they have, like normal kids."

"No lip-reading at all?" I questioned.

"No, we train them to listen. Teachers cover their mouths during the speech lessons," she said firmly. "Lip-reading will come naturally later when they become older." She added, "The vocal cords tend to be distorted if overemphasizing lip-reading; also, lip-reading distracts from the listening skills."

"How do I know this program is right for my son?" I asked.

"We will try it for one year. We would be able to tell whether this program is a good fit for him by then. If it's not, we'll discuss the options and refer him to other programs," she replied. "The listening skill is the hardest to acquire for deaf kids. But once they acquire it and learn to talk through that route, signing and lip-reading can be easily added on later. We will teach Teddy to talk and argue with you." She looked at Teddy and smiled fondly.

"Whatever it takes." The image of my son arguing with me was a vision of hope since the audiologist predicted that he would never call me "Mommy" verbally.

He must be able to call me "Mommy" before arguing with me!

I made my decision on the way home. *This was the program I wanted my son to be in*. I wanted him to know there was a thing called *sound*. I wanted him to be able to hear my voice. I wanted to be able to call him and warn him when he was in danger. I wanted him to be able to listen to music, the universal language.

Teddy was fitted with a set of powerful hearing aids. The process was taxing, from making the ear molds, to finding the right settings, and training him keep the hearing aids on. They were gigantic on his little ears; they flopped around. The combination of foreign objects hanging on his ears and the sound they generated, agitated him. I could imagine how confusing and frightening it was for him when his silent world was suddenly intruded on by noises. At first, he violently ripped off the hearing aids and threw them on the floor. I put thick cushions around his high chair to prevent the hearing aids from being damaged. We had to use surgical tape to secure them, and behavior modification to help him keep the aids on.

Majority of these events happened during my maternity leave following Victoria's birth. Juggling breastfeeding, and helping Teddy adapt to his aids, kept me busy. Trust me, there was not one dull moment during those days. Despite all that, I realized it was not an option for me to be a full-time, stay-at-home mother. We needed the group health insurance, through my employment, for Teddy's medical condition. There was no other viable option.

Teddy started his auditory-oral training at Oralingua School, attending two days a week in the beginning. I was told they adhered to Dr. Daniel Ling's theory and philosophy. We played the games with the six Ling sounds: [m], [ah], [oo], [ee], [sh], and [s]. For example, airplane goes [ah]; snake goes [s]; baby is sleeping [sh], etc. We covered our mouths, and Teddy had to listen and pick the right figure or picture card. When he did it correctly, he was rewarded with Cheerios. We talked to him whenever we were with him. We showed him all the environmental sounds: "Listen, telephone is ringing. Listen, water is running." We played the "listen to the doorbell" game. We said, "Up, up, up," as we picked him up from the high chair. We read picture books to him; we played music when our mouths went dry and our voices ran out. He was immersed in some sort of sound throughout the day. We had verbal diarrhea. Gradually, he attempted to say some words. The first word he said was "up" and then "Dada." I waited patiently until "MomMom" came later. I cried when it finally happened.

He called me "MomMom" with his voice!

Once he completed his potty training, he was in the auditory-oral school five mornings a week. He acquired vocabulary and learned simple sentences. His voice was fairly normal. However, his audiogram showed that many sounds fell off the speech banana, an area that represents the intensity and frequency of speech sounds in spoken language, despite wearing the powerful hearing aids; especially the sounds above frequency 2000 Hz. He complained that the right half of the piano keys were broken when I played the piano for him.

At the beginning of the 1990s, the FDA approved an electronic device to be implanted into prelingual profoundly deaf children, called the cochlear implant (CI). During a parenting meeting, Teddy's teacher mentioned the limited capacity of conventional hearing aids for Teddy's profound hearing impairment. She presented the potential benefits of the cochlear implant for his listening and language skill development. After a serious discussion of the risks, pondering the pros and cons of the procedure, and an intense fight with the insurance company, we—his parents, school teachers, and medical professionals—took a quantum leap. It was a collective, ambitious, and somewhat scary decision to move forward with the implant. I lost sleep for countless nights. The stress took a toll on me; I had frequent stomach aches.

Teddy was the first kid in his school to undergo the procedure with a multichannel implant. He received his first cochlear implant in his right ear in December of 1991. He was four and a half years old. Basically, twenty-two segments of electrodes were inserted into his cochlea—the inner ear. A receiver was embedded in the bone under the skin above the ear. Externally, there was a speech processor, a computer, connected to a coil, which magnetically attached to the receiver, and a microphone behind his right ear. The late Dr. William House, one of the pioneers of this device and procedure, performed the surgery.

One month later, he had his first "mapping," the procedure to determine the comfort and threshold levels of each electrode. The mapping was done several times during the first year to ensure the proper settings and provide him with optimal hearing. The drive to Dr. House's office in Newport Beach was long, and the traffic on SR 55 was horrendous, but I was hopeful that the CI would bring Teddy's hearing to a new level.

The hope sustained my sanity on those days.

In the beginning, he wore the speech processor in a pouch around his waist. That made him obviously different, because there was a long wire connecting the coil/microphone from his ear to the processor. We were told that rehabilitation was critical, because he needed to learn the new sounds. The sounds coming through the cochlear implant were digitalized; they would sound like Donald Duck talking or like someone speaking underwater—at least that's how the adult CI recipients described it. Since he was the first kid in his school and one of the few kids of his age nationwide who had undergone the procedure, Teddy was somewhat of an experiment for educators in the field at that time. His speech and listening skills progressed dramatically in one year. One day, he excitedly proclaimed that all the piano keys were okay while he used his index finger to tap the farthest right end of the keys. He was considered a successful case with CI back then.

Educators attributed his success to the intense pre-CI training; the hardware of his hearing and language systems (the auditory and language areas of his brain) had been installed, wired, and readied, and the CI just further activated the system. The sound through the right ear with CI, overpowered the left ear with the hearing aid. He stopped wearing the hearing aid on his left ear soon after the implant. I will elaborate on this issue in a later chapter.

Initially, friends and relatives had the impression that CI would provide perfectly normal hearing for him. They were frustrated when he appeared perplexed in certain environments. In reality, CI has its limitations; it did not give Teddy a bionic ear. It worked relatively well in a quiet environment. It certainly provided him with more sound-awareness, but the background noises had a tremendous effect on the quality and clarity of human voices. For example, he had difficulty carrying on a conversation in a restaurant. The lawnmower outside the classroom severely distorted and masked the teacher's voice. He had difficulty following the coach's instructions in outdoor team sports like Little League baseball. Multiple speakers at one time would throw him off entirely. We were told that continued rehabilitation after the CI surgery was critical, so the intense five-days-a-week auditory-oral training continued for several years. Regular audiologist visits to fine-tune his processor became part of his growing-up life. He took piano lessons to further enhance his sound and rhythmic awareness, and improve his fine motor skills.

As time passed, Teddy gradually picked up lip-reading skills naturally. It became obvious that he comprehended the content of conversation much better, when he combined the CI and lip-reading. He could even communicate somewhat in the swimming pool while his CI was off, though it was a struggle.

Teddy switched from the body-worn to a behind-the-ear processor in high school, which eliminated the long wire coming down from his ear to the waist. and made his wardrobe selections much more flexible. We had to upgrade the processor a few times through the years, due to advances in technology. Of course, like all electronic devices, the breakdown of the CI was inevitable. When that happened, it was a hassle for us and frustrating for him.

Based on the research, nearly forty percent of severely and profoundly deaf kids have received CI in recent years. The FDA has reduced the approval age to twelve months old, and loosened the restrictions on a candidate's criteria. More insurance companies authorized the CI procedures for young children and adults. Bilateral CI simultaneously implanted is a trend.

Teddy had the first generation of Nucleus 22-channel implanted in his right ear, and upgraded to a Nucleus 6 System processor recently.

In retrospect, the decision to have Teddy undergo the CI procedure was a tenuous one, filled with both hope and tremendous uncertainty. Did we play God in determining whether he could have access to the world of sound? Countless nights, I lay on the bed and stared at the ceiling, tossing and turning, wondering whether we had done the right thing for him. Would he appreciate the decision we'd made for him?

Recently, I had a chance to ask Ted whether

he would advise parents who just discovered they have a profoundly deaf child to consider CI, assuming the child is a good candidate. He firmly said, "Yes," but added, "Let the child have the free will to choose the mode of communication when he becomes mature enough." I assumed that was closure.

We have no regrets at this very moment, all things considered. This is all I can say.

CHAPTER 9

Social Skills Development

"I believe you learn social skills by mixing with people."

~Joe Morgan

I once learned that children born with genetic disorders or with special needs were considered demon-possessed in some cultures. They believed that those kids should be locked up and isolated from society. Fortunately, we are far away from that kind of ignorant mentality, for the most part. Yet, it remains a challenge to assist special needs children in developing the necessary social skills, and help them integrate as part of society. Of course, the nature of the child's disability is a factor. Besides, it is not so plain and easy to know when and how far we should push a child in this endeavor.

♥ Eichin's Story ♥

When we enrolled Teddy in the Oralingua School in Whittier, we were told that the school's ultimate goal was to help the students acquire the social skills to eventually be mainstreamed and integrated into society. Perhaps, since the initial outlook from the audiologist was so gloomy, we were skeptical. However, we were determined to work with the school to reach that goal.

Oralingua was a school for deaf children, but they did bring normal-hearing kids into the classroom regularly. Some of them were siblings of deaf students; others were the children or relatives of faculty members. That was called reverse mainstreaming. To get a sense of real society, parents signed up to host the students at their workplaces if it was permissible. The school provided an extensive curriculum that included field trips to the museum, aquarium, and amusement parks.

During one of the meetings with Teddy's classroom teacher when he was four years old, the teacher made a remark: "Your biggest challenge as Teddy's parents is not his deafness, but his way of doing things. He is the kind of kid who always wants to do things according to his own agenda. This may impede his social skills." At one point in time, he was even labeled as having a mild form of ADHD or autism. Then, we were told his IQ was above average. We tried not to get caught up in all these terms, labels, and diagnoses, and never put him on any medications. Deep inside, I knew it was just part of his personality, and I had to be patient working with him, and deal with it when he behaved inappropriately.

The reason I mention this is to illustrate the importance of understanding your kid's personality. Those words from the teacher were a bit baffling then; however, they served as a beacon, guiding me toward an understanding of Teddy's many awkward social behaviors, without sticking all kinds of labels on him.

Social skills involve interacting with others, following directions, and being aware of your surroundings. Teddy started kindergarten at partial mainstream. He attended the local public school a couple mornings a week. The resource teacher from Oralingua School would visit him and work with the public school teachers to evaluate his readiness. The first attempt did not go well, as he was too involved in his own agenda and wanted to do things in his own way. So, he was transferred back to Oralingua full time.

The second attempt was when he was in the first grade. Again, he would attend the local public school, Olita Elementary School, three to four mornings a week. The teachers from both Oralingua and Olita would monitor, evaluate, and guide him closely. He completely mainstreamed into Olita in the second grade. It was not clear-cut whether he was socially ready for mainstreaming, but he was obviously ready academically.

On the first day of school, Teddy, with his deafness and cochlear implant, was introduced to his new classmates. I was more nervous than he was that day. I remember putting a pack of implant batteries into the side pocket of his backpack. I pulled it in and out, in and out, several times, to ensure he remembered where the backup batteries were in case he needed them. The principal and classroom teacher were so supportive. We are indebted to them for what they did for Teddy.

To help him develop friendships, we bought the latest and most popular children's video games and movies, so he could invite his friends to the house on weekends. A birthday party was something he definitely needed to have. I intentionally took my turn carpooling with other parents two days a week, so I could observe how Teddy interacted with other kids and guide him as needed.

Despite all the efforts we made to assist him with social skills, the challenge of bullies persisted through junior high school. A funny-looking object hooked behind his right ear, with a wire hanging down from it, was conspicuous. Remember, that was before iPods and most of the other electronic gadgets we're all connected to today. He was a skinny little boy, and he started to have gray hair at a young age. Premature graying was part of Waardenburg syndrome. On top of all these, he wore a pair of bifocals to correct his *esotropia*, which caused his eyes to turn inward (also called "Wall Eyes' by some people.) We did sign him up for team sports, like baseball, but that did not work out.

Years later, he asked us to sign him up for Shaolin Kung Fu. He enjoyed it, and it built up his confidence tremendously. In retrospect, we should have started him in it at a much younger age, instead of trying many different sports. Even though Kung Fu is not a team sport, the confidence he gained from it benefited him in dealing with bullying, and in other areas of his social skills development.

Yes, each kid develops his social skills in a different way and at a different rate. We have to be patient and heedful as parents. You also need to include the child's personality into the equation. I hate to say it, but many times, it is all about trial and error. You can read all the parenting books, but not all the kids follow the textbook. Your child is a unique individual.

Do not beat yourself up or get frustrated if you find yourself constantly apologizing for your child's inappropriate social behaviors. Sometimes, a little sense of humor can lighten up the situation. I know it's easy to say but much harder to do.

CHAPTER 10

Working with School and Resource Teachers

"Education is a shared commitment between dedicated teachers, motivated students, and enthusiastic parents with high expectations."

~ Bob Beauprez

Every parent with a special needs child must be familiar with the Individualized Education Plan (IEP) process. A meeting is held at least once a year throughout your child's years of education. It can be intimidating, dreadful, and anguish-causing for many parents.

I want to share with you a fantastic article written by Jennifer Bollero entitled, *8 Steps to Better IEP Meetings: Play Hearts, Not Poker*. Ms. Bollero is an attorney, arbitrator, mediator, and loving mother of an autistic daughter. First, she explains what an IEP is.

> "The IEP meeting, required by federal statute, is convened at least once a school year to plan an educational program that is tailored to the needs of each disabled child. The child's "team" attends the meeting: teachers,

therapists, parents, school administrators, and any other invited parties."

These are the eight steps she listed about how to get the most out of the IEP. I encourage you to read the entire article.

http://www.wrightslaw.com/advoc/articles/iep.bollero.hearts.htm

1. Make every attempt to sustain relationships.

2. Keep the focus on the child's needs, not the district's resources or the parents' expectations.

3. Always provide "face-saving" ways out of dilemmas. Have a backup plan.

4. Build your record.

5. Walk a mile in the other side's moccasins.

6. Listen actively, especially to the things you do not want to hear.

7. Encourage everyone to love your child and then let them!

8. Have a little faith.

♥ Eichin's Story ♥

In the 1980s and 1990s, the majority of public deaf education was focused on sign language. However, we decided to go the oral route through a private school for Teddy. The tuition for Oralingua School was around $24,000 per year then, if my memory serves me correctly. In order for us to get funding from the district, we pursued the so-called legal way. We were told that we had to be our kid's advocate. We were quite naïve at the time, so we just followed the guidance of other parents who had been through the process.

Besides my husband and me, the meetings were usually attended by his teacher from Oralingua School, his speech therapist, his audiologist, a representative from the school district, and the mediator. I don't recall any major conflicts during these meetings, especially after Teddy received his cochlear implant. Since Teddy was one of the few kids who received Nucleus 22 right after the FDA's approval for kids with prelingual deafness, the school district was happy to leave Oralingua School in charge of coordinating his rehabilitation and education.

In addition to being hearing impaired, Teddy has a visual condition called *esotropia*. It's a form of strabismus which made his eyes turn inward. He did vision therapy at home and wore bifocal glasses to help strengthen his eyes and improve his hand-eye coordination. Since both his parents are in the eye care profession, his strabismus was part of the IEP. Teddy would have two strabismus surgeries later, one at the age of eleven, and another during college.

The IEP continued during his mainstream years. The services he received were speech therapy, and he had resource teachers to monitor his academic progress.

I would like to share my experience of working with the classroom teachers.

No matter how crazy my schedule was, I attended the Back to School Night at the beginning of each new school year. At the first one I attended, a parent raised a hand and asked, "I heard there is a kid with AIDS in this classroom. Should we be concerned about it?" At the time, the AIDS scare was at its peak, so Teddy's cochlear implant device—his hearing "aid"—was misinterpreted as AIDS in that parent's mind.

After that, I had a mission for Back to School Night. I made acquaintances with teachers. I prepared simple diagrams and provided information about cochlear implants and strabismus. I helped the teachers and other parents feel comfortable about Teddy's condition. Building good relationships with teachers is key to helping your kid to excel. I gave teachers all my contact information so they could reach me whenever they wanted or needed to do so. I never missed a teacher-parent meeting. I made the effort to express my appreciation during those special occasions and holidays—not to be a brownnoser, but to sincerely thank them for their support.

I thought of a couple instances to share here.

One time, I received a call from Teddy's math teacher. She was in tears. She could not understand why Teddy always fell asleep in her class, regardless of how hard she tried to keep him engaged. It turned out that her class was scheduled during the time the gardener worked outside on a section of lawn. The noise of the lawn mower, amplified through his CI processor, masked that teacher's voice. Perhaps, the sound was the exact frequency needed to trigger his brain to release the "doze off" chemical into his bloodstream. Once the teacher understood the situation, she did not take it personally any longer. Later, Teddy tried the FM system to combat the background noise in the classroom, but he disliked it.

On another occasion, the school nurse called me at work. She briefly explained to me that Teddy could not hear in the classroom because his CI processor was broken. Then she said, "Let me hand the phone to Teddy so you can talk to him." She obviously had not translated the classroom situation into the real-life situation. *How could he hear me on the phone if his CI processor was broken and he could not hear?* Teddy was probably the only deaf student she had ever encountered in her career at that point in time.

Regardless, I have found that it's much easier if you view the school teachers and administrators as your teammates and embrace them just as they are. You don't always have to agree with your teammates, but you are working together to achieve one goal: to win the game of helping your child reach his full potential.

CHAPTER 11

Surviving the Teenage Years

"Telling a teenager the facts of life is like giving a fish a bath."

~Arnold H. Glasow

Being a teenager is a period of confusion and uncertainty in a person's life. It's a time when you want to be included; you want to belong. And you want to be alone. You desperately want to blend in and stand out. You want to be treated as an adult, and you want to be taken care of like a child. You want the freedom, but dread the responsibilities. You cannot wait to grow up. Your parents are annoying, but you cannot live without them. Your emotions run up and down like a roller coaster or a raging river. As I look back at that period, I'm not sure I would want to go through it again if given the chance. With that said, I have an abundance of empathy for today's teenagers.

♥ Eichin's Story ♥

Before I dive into this section, I have to confess that I was not the most patient mother while my children were teenagers. I had empathy for them, but I lose sight of the big picture, and threw my sense of humor out the window more often than not. I spent much time mending the relationships.

From that point on, Teddy insisted on being called Ted. During those years, not only did he grow taller, but his gray hair became more noticeable. The premature graying definitely had a negative impact on his self-image.

Ted was a typical teenager in many ways. He got into trouble like many kids his age. Unfortunately, when things happened, he stood out. People would use phrases like, "That *deaf* boy got into trouble again!"

These were some major events during his teenage years.

He was suspended three times in junior high and high school. Every time he got suspended, I went bananas. The first time was because he did not follow a rule in biology class. The other two times were because he got into a fight with other kids. I took him to counseling. That was when he asked us to sign him up for a Kung Fu class. The fighting eventually stopped.

In the summer following tenth grade, he wore a black, long-sleeved, hooded sweatshirt with "Ninja" written at the front. He had a bet with friends that he could wear that sweatshirt through the entire Southern California summer. He did. He continued wearing that sweatshirt into the next school year. One day, he led a group of friends up onto the roof of the school. Of course, he got into trouble. When the principal asked him for an explanation, he simply said, "I am a Ninja." Eventually, he gave up that black sweatshirt, but it's still preserved in his closet even after all these years.

In the eleventh grade, Ted was invited to a friend's overnight birthday LAN party. He brought his own computer. However, he and a group of friends decided to visit another friend at midnight, and were caught by the police for violating the curfew law. He received a ticket, was summoned to court, and faced the judge. I sat on the bench with him as ordered, because he was a minor. He had the option of paying the fine or doing community service. He chose to do community service for several weeks. Truthfully,

I was grateful that he did dumb things like that while he was still living at home, so we could give him some guidance. It was not a pleasant event, but it certainly was good for him to experience the judicial system and realize that there are consequences for his actions.

A major goal for most teenagers is to earn their driver's license. The driver's license is seen as proof that you are a grown-up; you are independent. Ted took driver's education and obtained a learner's permit with no sweat. We figured it was better to have a professional driving instructor teach him how to drive properly and safely, so we hired a guy from a certified driving school. He was a big guy; you could easily imagine he played some sort of football in his youth. Ted was all pumped up to have two hours of driving lessons on the first day.

However, the instructor brought him back home after fifteen minutes. He said, "Mrs. Lim, your son should never drive on the road." He made no attempt to hide the trepidation in his voice. "He is a dangerous driver, and he might kill himself or someone else." He turned on his heel and left.

We wondered what had happened, but Ted walked straight to his room and locked himself in. After a week of avoiding the matter, he said to me, "Mom, I'd be real handicapped if I did not have a driver's license." Through our conversation, I finally got the details of what happened during his first behind-the-wheel driving lesson. Apparently, the rumbling of the car engine and the street noise masked the instructor's voice. In order for him to understand the instructor, Ted had to turn his head to read his lips. While he turned his head to read his lips, he turned the wheel at the same time and almost hit the car in the next lane.

Ted did some preparation before the next driving instructor was hired. This time, they established some hand signals before starting the engine. Basically, the instructor would point his right thumb to the right or his left thumb to the left to indicate which direction to turn. His index finger pointing forward told Ted to go straight. There were hand signals for slow down, go faster, keep the speed consistent. All these gestures were made within his field of vision so Ted could keep his eyes on the road and drive without turning his head. He passed his driver's license test on the second try. A few years later, he drove himself two thousand miles from Southern California to Chicago. On top of all this, Ted underwent a second cochlear implant surgery, and intensive rehab therapy afterward as a senior in high school. The surgery went smoothly. However, the second CI was declared a failure after two years of trying. The interval between the two CI surgeries was too long, and the sound perceived between the two ears was unable to integrate. He gave up the second CI eventually. As a mother, I was disappointed.

Ted graduated from high school at seventeen with an AP Scholar award. When "Pomp and Circumstance" played and the graduates marched in, my tears streamed down. I was so proud of him.

Surviving the teenage years is a challenge for all children and parents, but we survive anyway.

CHAPTER 12

Genetic Counseling and Sex Education

"Knowledge is love and light and vision."

~Helen Keller

Genetic counseling is the process of seeking advice from a genetic professional to determine your child's genetic condition, and the probabilities of future generations carrying the genes for particular inherited disorders. The tests are done by analyzing blood samples or body tissues.

Human genes are made up of DNA molecules, with forty-six chromosomes arranged in twenty-three pairs. Some genetic disorders are inherited from one or both parents; some are due to an error (mutation) in one gene, or even the variation of one piece of DNA in the process of cell division during conception or fetal development.

Currently, there are no definite genetic associations with some disorders, like autism spectrum disorder (ASD), attention deficit hyperactivity disorder (ADHD), or anxiety disorders. It is advisable to involve your child in the process of genetic counseling, if appropriate, and if he or she is cognitively capable.

Genetic counseling goes hand in hand with sex education and birth control. Some experts believe that sex education should start at home, as early as toddler-age, and definitely before puberty; even for children with congenital disabilities, and those who are developmentally and mentally disadvantaged. Since all human beings have sexual feelings and longings for intimacy, appropriate and individually-designed sex education can reduce or avoid the incidences of sexual abuse, unwanted pregnancy, sexual misunderstanding, and sexually transmitted diseases.

♥ Eichin's Story ♥

I admit that providing sex education to my kids was not one of my strengths as a parent. I could not recall my parents having ever talked to my brothers and me about sex when we were growing up. One summer, between my fourth and fifth grades, my parents did a renewal, remodel, and addition to our house, so my two brothers and I had to stay with my aunt. My aunt had four kids of her own and a bookshelf full of romantic and adult novels. I hid in the closet, embarrassed, my heart racing. I read the love stories and adult scenes, and that was how I obtained my sex education.

Due to background and cultural restraints, I missed many opportunities to provide sex education to my own kids. For example, I found Victoria sobbing in the restroom one day, her sweatpants soaking-wet. She was pre-kindergarten then.

"What's wrong, sweetheart?" I said.

"Teddy said he could stand up and pee. I wanted to show him I could do that too." She cried even harder.

It would have been a great opportunity for me to explain to my kids the anatomical differences between a boy and a girl, but all I said was, "You and Teddy are different. You have long hair and Teddy has short hair." I am a health-care provider with a solid background in human anatomy, biology, and physiology. Yet, when I had the perfect opportunity to talk to my own kids about "the birds and the bees," all I did was give them a lame answer. Part of it was due to my assumption that they were too young to have sex education. Through the years, I kept waiting for the "right time" to talk to them about sex.

I was prompted to do something about it, when one of the parents asked me whether I knew the boys were passing pornographic pictures in the restroom during recess, in seventh grade. I purchased a video recommended by one of the parenting magazines, titled *Love, Lust, Sex and Relationships*—or something like that. It was produced by a reputable agency, and talked about the responsibilities and consequences of actions. When I showed the video to my children, they rolled their eyes and snorted at me. To entice them, I flashed twenty-dollar bills, and basically bribed them to watch the entire movie. That video served as a vehicle for me to talk about some of the concerns. Of course, their responses consisted mostly of, "We know all about that already."

I knew they told their friends about it. When I went to pick up Teddy from school the next day, a couple of boys approached me.

"Mrs. Lim, can we come to your house to watch the movie?"

"What movie?" I asked.

"The sex movie. Ted said if we watch that movie, you will give us twenty dollars."

I checked the availability of sex education materials online recently, and discovered that there are some good-quality uploads on YouTube for various ages. They should be a great resource for parents who want to jump-start sex education at home.

Ted had asked me a couple times whether I had used alcohol or drugs when I was pregnant with him. He wanted to know why he had the Waardenburg gene. I assured him that I had been cautious, and had done everything right while carrying him. Since there was no family history of Waardenburg syndrome, we assumed Ted's condition was due to a mutation. Ted understood his condition, and realized that there's a fifty percent probability of his offspring carrying the gene. He is currently in a relationship with a lovely girl. We'll let him make the informed decision when that time comes.

CHAPTER 13

Occupational Choices

*"It's not what you achieve, it's what you overcome.
That's what defines your career."*

~Carlton Fisk

As parents of a special needs child, our ultimate goal is to bring up the child as an independent individual and a contributing citizen. Whether this goal can be achieved largely depends on the severity and the nature of the child's condition. We want to be hopeful and positive to help them reach their greatest potential, yet we need to be mindful of realistic expectations as well.

According to some reliable data, the average person changes jobs five to seven times in a lifetime. It's not easy to pin down an occupation and stay with it until retirement. There are some career aptitude tests and personality tests available that can evaluate an individual's strengths, weaknesses, and restrictions, to narrow down a person's occupational choices.

Also, social workers from the Department of Rehabilitation are helpful in assisting in occupational guidance. Even so, nothing is one hundred percent when it comes to a person's career.

♥ Eichin's Story ♥

Ted did more than one hundred hours of volunteer work at a hospital during high school, and he enjoyed it very much. However, he was uncertain about his real passion at that time. In twelfth grade, he took a Career Assessment Inventory test through the Department of Rehabilitation. The Occupational Scales showed broad themes for him; it was not specific enough. Around that time, he wanted to apply to the Air Force Academy, so I took him to meet with the recruiter. That did not work out.

Immediately after high school, he was admitted to the University of California at Irving (UCI), majoring in philosophy, with the intention of pursuing law or a related field later. Two years later, he decided to take a break to do some soul searching. He took two terms off and worked as a cook at a fast food chain. He reentered UCI and changed his major to economics. Despite changing majors, he worked in a clinical lab and performed research with a professor for four years. He had one research paper accepted and presented at an international conference.

After receiving his degree, Ted worked at a reputable financial institution. Even though electronic communication is popular, effective telephone communication remains critical in the financial industry. Even with a cochlear implant, it's a real challenge for Ted to carry on conversations via telephone, or in a noisy environment. He has a nice voice, and his speech is easy to understand, but not perfect. Also, he found out banking was not his aspiration. He veered toward a career in personal care, where face-to-face communication would be most useful.

Since Ted is a strong-willed individual, we let him decide his career route. We understand that nothing is more important than having passion for your job. Some people find their passion right away; others have to explore their options before finding the right one.

Once he decided to change careers, he enrolled in science classes at a local college and completed the prerequisite courses and Graduate Record Examinations (GRE) for graduate school. He shadowed his mentor in the hospital for quite a while. After a couple of years of intensive preparation, he completed his application process. However, he failed the first two interviews for the graduate school admission. It was devastating.

The interval between the second and third interviews was seven months. A dreadful wait!

As of this moment, Ted has been accepted and is enrolled into the Doctorate of Physical Therapy program at a reputable university. I could not hold back my tears when the acceptance news arrived. It has been a long and winding road. I am so proud of him.

CHAPTER 14

Time to Let Go

"We must be willing to let go of the life we have planned, to have the life that is waiting for us."

~E. M. Forster

Almost all mothers have the desire to be a good mother. Part of being a good mother is to oversee and be involved in every aspect of the child's life. This is a belief that a mother holds on to from the day she learns that she's carrying a fertilized egg in her womb.

I've heard it said that if you loved someone, you have to let them go... to know if they were ever truly yours to begin with.

This is not about letting go of our love for our children. It's about letting THEM go; letting them become independent. It doesn't mean that we'll stop caring for them. We're just not supposed to smother them with our love.

Surely, we can let go of our children and watch them soar, but that doesn't lessen our love for them. How could a mother ever let go of her motherly love? If anything, it grows even stronger as we watch our children become confident, successful, independent adults.

♥ Eichin's Story ♥

I was tending to the after-dinner mess one night when Ted came to me. He was a sophomore in high school.

"Mom, I need to talk to you about something."

When he approached me to talk about something, I knew it would not be a casual conversation. Something had been brewing in his mind for a while, and he had an agenda. I gave him a nod.

"Mom, I have too much of you in me," he said, and the warmth of pride surged up within me. "We need to change that, Mom."

The bubbly feelings burst instantly. "What're

you talking about?"

"Mom, you need to let me grow up the way I want to. You need to trust me. Let me learn from my own mistakes if I fall," he pleaded.

I could not let my kids fall. *What if they never get back up?* It was a horrendous thought.

"You really need to find something to do so you don't focus on Victoria and me so much," he said.

I got the picture. I was the monkey on their backs. They wanted to get rid of the monkey breathing down their necks all the time. His words were not easy to swallow, but I took them to heart. I realized that I had to divert my attention to somewhere else, but where?

There were options. I pondered hard.

First, I joined dance aerobics classes at the city community center twice a week. I moved my body with the music, and the workout and sweat delighted me. Then, I undertook something mentally challenging. I signed up for online real estate broker license classes. I gave myself an aggressive goal: to complete the nine courses and pass the licensing exam in twelve months. It was a bit out of reach, but I gave it a shot.

Even though they were online courses, I bought the physical books. I sat at the dining table and dove in, headfirst, nightly. Once I finished a course, I would go online to take the test and receive the certificate. *One course at a time*, I told myself. My family was aware of my endeavor and had been supportive, but I made them swear to keep it a secret.

Twelve months later, I passed the California real estate broker licensing exam on the first try. I was jubilant and empowered to no end—not because I passed on the first try, but because of the acknowledgment that my brain could absorb, process, and still retain so much new information, especially given the chaotic nature of our lives and the distractions of my day job. My children were preparing to take the ACT and the SAT at that time. My success in passing the licensing exam seemed to inspire my kids, and I'd like to think they respected me more because of it. Also, it was proof that I'd listened to Ted's advice and respected his opinion. I had, indeed, "found something to do" for myself. I have managed to keep my real estate broker license up-to-date through the years.

My next venture was signing up for the online

Certified Financial Planner (CFP) program. The list of required courses was intimidating, and it was a real struggle to put aside my self-doubt and open the first page. I completed the required courses in about one year but, after careful consideration, decided to forego the licensing exam due to the onerous demands of maintaining the CFP license from year to year. Even so, the knowledge I gained from the courses expanded my horizons and helped me to be more confident when discussing my financial affairs with my planner.

I was also proud to know that I could put aside my role as the monkey on the kids' backs.

After both of my children went to college, I furthered my adventures in acting and writing. I refrained from texting my kids more than a couple of times a week. We were under the agreement that they would contact us when they needed us. Trust me, it was not an easy transition.

Instead of suffocating my children with my love, being a helicopter mom, I gave them room to breathe, to find their own way. Because of my genuine love for them, I listened to my kids' concerns, took their words to heart, adjusted my behavior, and gave them the space they desired. As Ted said, I needed to find something to occupy my mind. And I did, though that overwhelming motherly love still occupies my heart. I have to admit that it's not an overnight, once-and-for-all process, and I'm still learning—we all are.

But I do know for a fact that dumping all my focus on them was not healthy for any of us.

CHAPTER 15

It's Okay if Things Don't Turn Out as You Expected

"No one is so brave that he is not disturbed by something unexpected."

~Julius Caesar

As they say, we would not have disappointments if we did not have expectations. Are we discrediting our noblest living anchor, hope, if we become afraid of setting expectations? What a shallow life it would be if we forego the hope!

We have hope. We have expectations for our kids, especially the ones whom we have devoted so much of our time and energy to bring out their best. However, we cannot hold ourselves hostage or beat ourselves up if things don't turn out the way we hoped they would. No one is perfect; no relationship is perfect. No matter how hard we try, we can never be perfect parents or have perfect relationships with our kids.

♥ Eichin's Story ♥

I have always told myself that I had to love both of my children equally, and hold the same expectations for them from day one. It's true that I have never favored one child over the other. However, it was inevitable that I had to spend much more time with Teddy throughout his childhood, than with Victoria. I had to take him to see specialists, the audiologists, and the speech therapists. His several invasive surgeries were heart-wrenching. The rehabilitation and follow-up visits after the surgeries demanded more time in doctors' offices and traveling in the car together.

Ted moved out of the house once he enrolled at the college. The University of California at

Irving was about a forty-minute drive from home. He eagerly moved out, and we thought it was a good thing for him to learn to be independent. But, oh how I missed him! His absence created a huge void, and I found myself making up reasons to see him. Our visits usually occurred on Sundays. I didn't need to spend the whole day with him; all I wanted was to have dinner with him. That's all. Not because I didn't trust him to take care of himself or wanted to baby him. I just wanted to spend time.

The desire to see him for Sunday dinner continued, and became a pleasant part of our routine. During one of those dinners—Ted had graduated and was working for a financial institution in Orange County at the time—he dropped a bomb on me.

"Mom, I quit my job and am moving to Chicago," he said.

"Why? When? Chicago?" My vision blurred and I fought the urge to vomit.

"Mom, I need to move out of Southern California. You are so overprotective of me."

I thought I'd made a great effort not to be the monkey on his back. I saw myself in the guide-and-support role, as a good mother is supposed to be. I didn't think I was being overprotective. Apparently, it was still not good enough for him. His need for independence ran much deeper and stronger than I'd ever imagined.

A few weeks later, he moved boxes of books and other personal stuff back home. Then, he loaded the rest of his belongings into his Toyota Corolla.

"Bye, Mom," he said and gave me a hug.

I collapsed after watching him drive off alone. Night after night, until he arrived in Chicago safely, my pillow was soaked with tears. I thought I had overcome being an overprotective mother years ago. I had modified my behavior, and done the right things for him since then. *Hadn't I? Have I been doing the wrong things all along? Was I a failure as his mother?* These pernicious questions lingered for months.

Now, however, I have turned a corner. I can see things from a different perspective. I am happy that he wants to accomplish things by himself. Did I not want him to be an independent man? His ability to do so is a sign that I've done my job well. There is a fine line between being overprotective of your child—something easy to do, especially when that child has special needs—and being an attentive, loving mother. It's a challenge to find the balance, even when guided by the noblest intentions.

CHAPTER 16

Motherhood Never Ends.
Give Yourself a Pat on the Back.

*"Optimism is the faith that leads to achievement.
Nothing can be done without hope and confidence."*

~Helen Keller

We need to learn to let go, to accept our kids as they are, even when things do not turn out as we expected. It is important to understand that letting our children go does not mean quitting our jobs as mothers, or loving them any less. Our job is to help them strengthen their wings, and guide them toward the right path, so they can soar from the nest and fly off into the world on their own. At the end of the day, we need to reward ourselves, and give ourselves a pat on the back for a job well done.

Motherhood is a lifetime engagement. It is not easy to be a mother, and we are doing a fantastic job. How marvelous we are! We all know there will be something else waiting for us tomorrow—good or bad or horrible—but we will have the strength to deal with whatever comes our way.

Yes! We can make it through.

♥ Eichin's Story ♥

Ted informed me a month ago that he would be coming home to attend a friend's wedding. Actually, he was one of the groomsmen. Then, he added that he would be bringing a girl home and would like for her to stay at the house. More precisely, he was bringing his girlfriend home to meet us! We were excited.

It was a short stay for them, but we liked her a lot. She seemed to have her own unique way of communicating with him, and she appreciates who he is.

Sending them off at John Wayne Airport, watching them stroll toward the gate together, a knot formed in my throat. I swallowed hard, took a deep, slow breath, and blinked back my tears.

Yes, I still wish he'd move back to Southern California. I miss him a lot. No one knows what the future holds, but I have confidence that he will be okay no matter where he is.

I am so proud to be his mother.

Thank you for reading *A Mother's Heart*

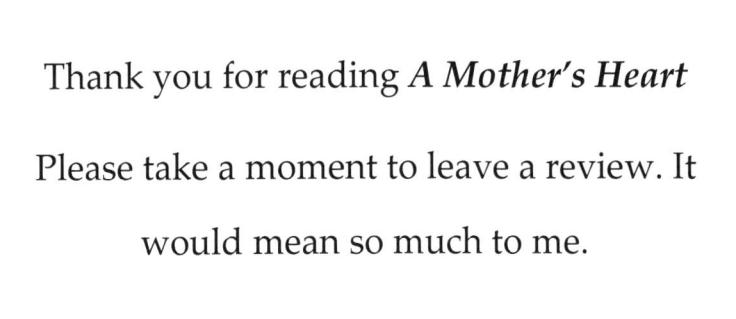

Please take a moment to leave a review. It would mean so much to me.

Download Part 1 of the Romantic and Inspiring Novel, FLIPPING.

bestread.net/flipping

Life can flip in the blink of an eye...

"Chang-Lim writes in a simple, direct prose style that seems to channel the matter-of-fact diligence of her characters ... quick little scenes that guilelessly propel the plot ..." - Kirkus Review

But Love will not be denied...

an uplifting novel of love

FLIPPING
FLIPPING
FLIPPING

EICHIN CHANG-LIM
EICHIN CHANG-LIM
EICHIN CHANG-LIM

www.eichinchanglim.com

About the Author

Dr. Eichin Chang Lim is an optometrist by day, an author by night, a wife, and a mother to 2 children. She and her husband have a private optometry practice in Los Angeles and lives in Orange County, CA.

Eichin modeled during college in Taiwan and was in several short films, including the comedy Indy/feature film "Winning Formula" as a supporting role. Besides acting and writing, she loves opera, classical music and a big bear hug.

Learn more about the author at:
www.eichinchanglim.com
Connect on Twitter: **@EichinChangLim**

Made in the USA
San Bernardino, CA
13 December 2018